Becoming Your Own Boss: Learn How to Fight Chaos Brought on by ADHD and Succeed in Home Business Ventures

Bring your business ideas to life by learning how to run a successful business from your own home.

J Quill.

Table of Contents

J Quill.	0
Table of Contents	1
CHAPTER 1: UNDERSTANDING THE BASICS OF ADHD	**4**
Symptoms of ADHD	4
The Subtypes of ADHD	5
CHAPTER 2: HAVE THE RIGHT SET OF TOOLS AND EQUIPMENT FOR THE FIGHT	**9**
Organize Your Thoughts and Ideas with Colored Pens and Sticky Notes	9
Jot Down Ideas Before You Forget Them with Dry Boards and More	10
Keep Everything Together with an Almighty Planner	11
CHAPTER 3: PRIORITIZING TASKS TO BE COMPLETED EACH DAY	**13**
Assess Your Day Afterwards to Gain Insight as to How Time Was Spent or What Can Be Done Better Next Time	15
Make Note to Avoid Distractions and Other Tasks at All Tasks Until Priority Tasks Are Completed	16
CHAPTER 4: CREATING A DISTRACTION-FREE HOME OFFICE ENVIRONMENT	**18**
Section Off Space Specifically for Work Purposes	18
Natural Lighting Improves Productivity and Energy Levels	20
The Right Temperature Can Keep You Focused and Alert	21

Get Rid of Distractions for a Quiet Work Environment	23
CHAPTER 5: TAKING CONTROL OF YOUR DAY BY KEEPING TRACK OF THE TIME	**25**
Keep Lots of Clocks Around Your Office	25
Keep Track of Progress with Alarms	26
Hire a Personal Assistant	27
CHAPTER 6: GETTING EXTERNAL HELP	**29**
Attend Counselling Sessions, Particularly Ones Aimed at Cognitive Behavioral Therapy	29
Group Therapy Gives You the Support You Need	31
Try Prescription Medications -- They Help!	32
CHAPTER 7: REMOVING PAPERWORK AND CLUTTER ON A SCHEDULE	**36**
Set Up a Schedule	36
Purchase Several Cabinets and Bins for Sorting Paperwork Based on Importance	37
Shred Anything that You Don't Need	38
Take the Opportunity to Also Clean the Office	38
Last Resort -- Hire a Professional Cleaner or Maid	39
CHAPTER 8: CLEARING YOUR MIND BY SCHEDULING TIME TO REST	**40**
Schedule Specific Break Times Using a Pomodoro	40
Get Some Exercise In-Between Your Work Day	41
Create a Calming Station for When Work Gets Hectic	42
CHAPTER 9: TAKING NOTES DURING MEETINGS	**45**
Record All Meetings and Phone Conversations to Go Over at a Later Time	45
Jot Down Important Notes and Make Them Concise	47

CHAPTER 10: EATING RIGHT TO HAVE THE ENERGY YOU NEED 48
    Drink a Cup of Coffee Each Morning Before Work   48
    Avoid Eating Sugary Foods and Sweets   49
    Eat Plenty of Protein   49
    Get Enough Energy for the Day with a Healthy and Balanced Breakfast   50

CHAPTER 11: DRESSING FOR SUCCESS   **51**
    Lay Out Several Outfits Ahead of TIme   51
    Stick to Minimalistic Palettes and Designs   52
    Create a Strict Dry-Cleaning or Laundry Schedule   53
    Buy Clothes from Stores that Organize Clothes Based on Shade and Color   53

CONCLUSION   **56**

CHAPTER 1: UNDERSTANDING THE BASICS OF ADHD

Small businesses are becoming the bread and butter of the U.S. economy. If you've got a great idea that you believe will take off, you can easily start your own small business at home. Becoming your own boss and getting everything done in a productive manner is not easy however when you're battling with ADHD every day.

It's easy to get overwhelmed by chaos, distractions and hyperactivity. Symptoms of ADHD can lead you astray and prevent your business from succeeding. Understanding the nuts and bolts of ADHD and how to conquer the chaos that it brings might be just what you need to ensure success. It's vital that you face your struggles with ADHD head on in order to free yourself from its grasp.

Symptoms of ADHD

If you haven't gotten diagnosed by a medical professional, that's the first step you should take in your battle against this neurobiological disorder. ADHD is not a disease. It's simply a disorder that affects the biology of your nervous system in a way that negatively impacts abilities related to executive function and self-regulation. According to Brain and Behavior Research Foundation, common symptoms of ADHD include:

- Forgetfulness;
- Inability to perform activities that require sustained mental effort;
- Difficulty organizing tasks;
- Hyperactivity;
- Being easily distracted or having an inability to concentrate or stay focused;
- Impulsive decision making; and,
- Difficulties following directions.

Those struggling with ADHD have difficulties with performing executive function. This includes tasks that require planning, strategizing, organizing, goal settings and paying attention to details.

The Subtypes of ADHD

ADHD comes in all shapes and sizes. Most medical professionals categorize ADHD into 3 distinct subtypes: the hyperactive or impulsive subtype, the inattentive subtype and the combined subtype. Those with hyperactive or impulsive subtype ADHD exhibit incessant and impulsive physical, mental and verbal activity without considering the consequences. Those with inattentive subtype tend to live in their own world and are prone to activities like daydreaming, and those that struggle with combined subtype ADHD possess symptoms that fall under both categories.

It can be difficult to pinpoint exactly which subtype you fall into. Generally speaking, most people exhibit symptoms from both the hyperactive or impulsive subtype and the inattentive subtype, which puts them in the combined subtype. Let's take a further look into the differences of each subtype, and how they may affect your ability to run a successful home business.

Below is a checklist that might help you determine which subtype you fall into. Check the symptoms that you exhibit to determine whether you fall into one subtype more than the other or whether you show a combination of symptoms from both subtypes.

Hyperactive or Impulsive Subtype	**Inattentive Subtype**
• Difficulties relaxing	• Difficulties paying attention to detail
• Prone to fidgeting, such as twitching or swinging their feet, during meetings or when performing activities that require sustained mental focus	• Tendency to make careless mistakes
• Constantly blurt out and interrupt others	• Feel sluggish more constantly than usual in

	comparison to others
• Tendency to overeat and overspend	• Have poor memory and constantly forget where they place things
• Often leaves a trail of stuff everywhere	• Are easily distracted

By getting diagnosed and further understanding the subtype of ADHD that affects you, you'll gain a better understanding of how this neurobiological disorder has prevented you from accomplishing your dreams and goals in the past. ADHD doesn't have to be a pest. It doesn't have to cause you to procrastinate and put off important work meetings that are preventing your business from growing and expanding. In fact, many geniuses have been diagnosed by this condition. If you learn how to manage the chaos that ADHD brings, you can subdue the symptoms and take full advantage of all of the benefits that ADHD has to offer.

One of the main benefits of ADHD is being able to think outside the box and coming up with creative ideas. This can help you rank your business above competitors. Still, learning how to manage ADHD symptoms is key to unlocking all of that creative and power that you secretly hold within. Once you can reign in the negative symptoms, you will have the ability to fully explore all of the joys that ADHD has to offer. In fact, after this book, you might find that ADHD is a gift rather than curse, as it can help you tackle difficult obstacles from different angles. It can help you make your business stand out from your competition. All you have to do is free yourself from its shackles.

CHAPTER 2: HAVE THE RIGHT SET OF TOOLS AND EQUIPMENT FOR THE FIGHT

Fighting symptoms of ADHD is not as easy as it looks, and chances are that you won't succeed without the right tools and equipment. Luckily, you don't need high-tech equipment to beat ADHD. In fact, you'll find all that you need at your local stationary store or even online. Although apps on your phone and other electronic devices can be a lot of help, most people with ADHD find that they respond better to physical stimuli. Writing everything down sticks better than typing it out. Here are several tools you'll need to get started and to turn your business ideas into reality.

Organize Your Thoughts and Ideas with Colored Pens and Sticky Notes

It's easy to let your mind wander and forget what's important. If you get easily distracted, it's critical that you can group similar thoughts together. It's easy to see which ideas or tasks are similar to one another from just a glance by categorizing them using colors. Vital tools to combating symptoms of ADHD include colored pens and colored sticky notes. Organize your thoughts based on colors, and you'll find that you'll also be able to focus much more easily.

For example, jot down business ideas related to product design with a purple colored pen and ideas or tasks related to finances with a green colored pen. You can even use color coded pens or color coded sticky notes to organize lists based on importance. Tasks or items that are more important should be written in red whereas tasks or items that are less important should be written using colors that are less bold, like orange or even pink.

Keeping various colored pens together can be difficult for someone with ADHD. It's not unusual to leave a pen on the counter after you write down some notes. To prevent yourself from having to waste time looking all over the place for the right colored pen, choose multi-colored pens that contain multiple colored ink cartridges in one place. You'll never have to worry about losing your pens again. For good measure, keep several pens around.

Jot Down Ideas Before You Forget Them with Dry Boards and More

Have you ever had a wonderful idea, but then completely forgot about what you were thinking about just moments later? Unfortunately, that's how ADHD minds work. It's not unusual for your thoughts to race around quickly, jumping from one idea to the next. If you don't want to let some great ideas go to waste, decorate your home office with dry boards, sticky notes and even chalkboards everywhere. This will allow you to easily write down ideas as they come to mind. Never forget a great idea again.

Look for dry boards that are made specifically from porcelain. These dry boards tend to last the longest time and can withstand years of abuse without any problem. You should hang dry boards not only in your home office, but also throughout your home as well. Hanging a dry board in the shower might not be a bad idea. You never know when an idea might come to you. If possible, look for dry boards that come with different colored pens that have magnets attached to them. The magnets allow the pens to be attached directly onto the dry boards. You can use different colored pens to help organize your thoughts and maintain focus.

Tip: The less porous the surface of the dry board is, the better. These dry boards tend to stand up to years of abuse much more easily and will be easy to clean.

Keep Everything Together with an Almighty Planner

If you have ADHD, a planner is perhaps one of the most useful tools you can have. Look for a compact planner that you can bring along with you just about anywhere. You want to find a planner that you like, as you want to resort to using one planner only. It's a good idea to choose one with refillable pages. Get a good look at your month, week and day by choosing a monthly, weekly and daily planner. Place the planner at the same spot on your desk and make sure to check it whenever you get up or sit down.

Write down your chores for each day in the daily section and main events in the monthly sections. The monthly section of the planner should give you a brief idea of what you can expect for the entire month. The weekly section should aim to accomplish a certain goal and the daily section should break down your goal into accomplishable tasks. Look for planners that not only have "to-do" lists, but also other organizers as well to make your life more organized. The more organized you are, the more focused you will be at growing and expanding your business.

Use the planner to make lists and to write down important tasks and events. It's important that you get a clear picture of your objectives, goals and plans. Try out different planner styles to figure out what works best for you.

When writing down tasks that need to be completed in a planner, you should try to stick to a schedule or a routine. A schedule or routine can really help keep you focused and give you the jumpstart that you need in your day.

CHAPTER 3: PRIORITIZING TASKS TO BE COMPLETED EACH DAY

It's easy to let hyperactivity or inattentiveness get the better of you and take full control of your day. If you struggle with ADHD, your mind can easily overpower you, and you can easily get distracted when attempting a single task. This might prevent you from accomplishing the most important tasks first. When you enter your home office every day, the first thing you should do is sit down and make a list of all of the tasks you need to and want to complete. Next, prioritize the tasks into 3 different subgroups: urgent, important and can wait.

Urgent tasks are tasks that *absolutely* have to be completed by the end of the day. For example, you might have to contact a supplier in order to restock your inventory immediately, as you have back orders. You don't want your customers or clients waiting. Important tasks are tasks that you want to complete by the end of the day, but the completion of these tasks can wait for a day or two. Tasks that are marked 'can wait' are ones that don't really have a due date at all. Avoid labelling all tasks as urgent or important. You want to keep as few tasks in these sections as possible in an attempt to narrow down your focus. You can further prioritize the tasks in each group based on their importance.

For example, let's say that you have to complete the following tasks:
1. Call a specific supplier by the end of the day to restock, as you have back orders;
2. Pay a bill by the end of the week;
3. Call a customer back in regards to a question they had about a certain product;
4. Name a new product that is going to be released in the near future; and,
5. Promote your products by tweeting customers that follow your company.

You might determine that calling the supplier and the customer back is of huge importance. This means that you should categorize these tasks as urgent. Paying the bill and promoting your product might be something you want to get done by the end of the day although there's no harm in pushing these tasks back by a day or two. As a result, they are important. The release of the new product might not have been set yet, so you might label the task as 'can wait'. You should organize the tasks out by reorganizing them in a list like the following. .

Urgent	Important	Can wait
1. Call the supplier to restock 2. Call the customer back	1. Promote product with tweet 2. Pay bill	1. Come up with a name for the new product

You should also prioritize the tasks based on importance and try to go down the list throughout the day by tackling the most urgent tasks tasks first. After completing urgent tasks, work your way towards important tasks before finishing up your day by tackling tasks you've deemed can wait.

TIp: Schedule similar tasks together, so that you can get similar things completed at the same time without any distractions. For example, you should try to make all of your calls at the same time or pay all of your bills at the same time. This helps waste less time, and will also help keep you more focused on the tasks you have.

Assess Your Day Afterwards to Gain Insight as to How Time Was Spent or What Can Be Done Better Next Time

At the end of the day, assess how your day went and whether you accomplished each task successfully. Reflect on how time was spent and whether you could've multi-tasked on gotten several tasks completed within the same time. For example, when you're on hold with the supplier, you could've easily signed in to online banking and paid the bill.

Purchase a journal for you to take notes on every day. Summarize your reflections, and try to remove all of the negative points a day at a time. Don't give up. You'll get the hang of it soon. Try not to regurgitate all of your points on the page. Create some type of template that will allow you to easily go over your reflections and figure out what works for you and what doesn't. Try out the following template if you don't know where to start.

Task or Activity	Time of Day Started	Length of Time It Took to Complete	Observations or Reflections
Example: Packed orders to be shipped today	9:30 am	30 minutes for 10 orders total	Would have been quicker if I printed the shipping labels first before packaging the orders
Example: Called the manufacturer to talk about using different type of fabric	11:30 am	45 minutes	Was on hold for an incredibly long time. I could have answered emails from customers and clients in the meantime

Make Note to Avoid Distractions and Other Tasks at All Tasks Until Priority Tasks Are Completed

Keep your lists of tasks to a minimum. If you find your list to be relatively wrong, try to accomplish only the tasks listed in urgent first or urgent and important first. The tasks listed in other subcategories are considered to be distractions and will prevent you from getting the important things done.

Rumor has it that even Warren Buffett uses this strategy. He makes a list of 25 tasks, and circles the top 5 tasks that he prioritizes. He'll focus all of his attention in getting the top 5 tasks completed during the day, and will do all that he can to avoid the other 20 tasks. Try this tactic out yourself as well to see whether it helps you zone in your focus and concentration.

CHAPTER 4: CREATING A DISTRACTION-FREE HOME OFFICE ENVIRONMENT

The environment which you work in plays a huge role on how productive you can be, so don't overlook how you set up your home office. You don't have to necessarily splurge in order to design a home office that helps you manage your symptoms. You just need to make sure that the environment is free of distractions, lest your mind decides to start wandering off to the unknown.

Section Off Space Specifically for Work Purposes

It's not unusual for those with ADHD to get easily distracted by stimuli in the nearby environment. One minute you might be sitting down to get some work done and the next you might be looking at toys that your kids left on the floor or the new rug that you just purchased, but isn't sure whether it goes with the room or not.

Ideally, you should designate a specific room in your house as the office. Keep any appliances, equipment or items that don't belong out. If you don't have a spare room in your house, you can try sectioning off some space in a room to transform into a home office. Make sure that you let other people in the household know that the space is designated specifically for work. Don't let your spouse, children or even friends launder around in your home office if it's not necessary to create a zenful space.

If you can't find a spare room to turn into a home office, section off some space in a room that will be relatively quiet. For example, consider sectioning off space in your bedroom. Avoid rooms that can get rowdy and loud, like your children's playroom. You can section off a certain area of the room using several techniques, such as:
- Installing ceiling mount curtains to section off your own private space in the middle or corner of the room;
- Putting up book shelves in order to create boundaries;
- Using wall dividers that can be folded away for convenience; and,
- Fixing fabric panels that can even double up as a projection screen when working.

Tip: Measure the dimensions of the office furniture, like the desk and the cabinets, to determine just how much space you'll need to section out for your home office. You want to know the precise measurements ahead of time before you install anything; otherwise, you run the risk of having too little space to successfully run your business from. It's best to give yourself more space than necessary, so that you won't feel crowded.

Natural Lighting Improves Productivity and Energy Levels

It's easy to feel discombobulated when you're stuck in a dim room. Your mind will have difficulty focusing and concentrating on tasks, and you'll feel extra sluggish throughout the entire day, which will cause you to become even more unproductive. Insufficient lighting has also been found to lead to migraines and eye strains. This is due to the fact that dim lighting basically forces your eyes to work harder throughout the day. You'll find yourself easily fatigued and burnt out if the lighting in your office is not ideal.

Natural lighting is most ideal for improving overall productivity and increasing energy levels throughout the day. Studies have found that natural lighting can do wonders in lifting the spirits of employees and keeping them productive and focused on the tasks at hand. In fact, the studies found that employees who were exposed to natural lighting [were 18% more productive](). If possible, create your home office in a room with many large windows. You want to let as much natural light inside the office as possible, so that you'll continue to feel rejuvenated and refreshed throughout the day.

If there aren't enough windows or you simply live in a dreary place without much sun, brighten up the rooms using as many LED light bulbs as possible. The LED light bulbs expose you to blue light, which can improve your performance when performing or completing important tasks. Avoid incandescent light bulbs as much as possible, as they are prone to making dull buzzing sounds that can be quite distracting if you have ADHD.

Install plenty of overhead light fixtures throughout your home office whenever possible. If you don't want to call in an electrician to modify the room, you can also get away with purchasing light fixtures, like lamps or desk lights. Floor lamps offer a significant amount of ambient lighting, and are a great choice. You can find many models and designs online and at your local furniture stores. Choose ones that are adjustable, so that you can control where the light shines.

Tip: Working by a window is not only a great way to expose yourself to more natural sunlight, but it can also help you absorb vitamin D. Vitamin D, also known as the sunshine vitamin, has been linked to reducing risk of depression and disease. Getting sufficient quantities of vitamin D can help elevate your mood, and also help you lose weight as well. It's absolutely a win-win situation. Make sure you choose a window that isn't facing a busy street, as you might get distracted by the events unfolding outside of the window throughout the day.

The Right Temperature Can Keep You Focused and Alert

Your body automatically regulates its temperature unbeknownst to you. You're usually not even aware of all that your body does to keep itself at an ideal temperature. On top of spending some time making sure that your home office has sufficient light, it's also important to consider how well-insulated the room is or whether it has climate-control features, like a trustworthy HVAC system that will regulate and maintain the room temperature at optimal levels. If not, consider purchasing a portable air conditioning system or even a heater.

When installing an air conditioning system or even a heater, the placement of the HVAC system is crucial. For one, you need to make sure that it is installed in a place that cannot be obstructed by furniture or other objects that you might mindlessly place in front of the ducts. Second of all, you should look for a unit that is relatively quiet and noise less. The less noise, the better, as you'll have less distractions to be worried about. Last but not least, an energy efficient HVAC system with an efficient filter can remove the majority of airborne particles and pollutants in the air being circulated in the office. Better air quality equals to higher comfort. You'll also reduce your risk of getting allergies.

While there isn't a definitive temperature that works for everyone, Cornell University has established that warmer office temperatures tend to lead to higher productivity and performance. By increasing the office temperature from 68 degrees Fahrenheit to 77 degrees Fahrenheit, participants in the study exhibited a typing output increase of 150%. They also made 44% less errors. You'll have to play around with the temperature settings to determine what's most comfortable and what works best for yourself bearing in mind that the ideal office temperature will differ from person to person. If you want to save some money on heating costs, consider wearing layers of clothing to keep you warm throughout the day, and to regulate your body temperature.

Get Rid of Distractions for a Quiet Work Environment

Buckle down and get work done by getting rid of distractions to create a quiet work environment that is free of any additional distractions. Turn off your phone or send all calls to voicemail, turn off email notifications and even put up a sign if necessary to let others know that you are not to be disturbed during certain hours. During these hours, try to do nothing more, but focus on your work.

Make a thorough sweep of your home office to determine whether there is anything that you might find distracting. Get rid of it all. You'll have to do some trial and error here to determine what works for you and what doesn't work for you. If other family members are going to be at home as well, consider putting up some signs to let them know that they are in a 'quiet zone'. You can even set hours for when your family members can come to you with problems that are not considered to be emergencies. If your office is close to a street, you might even want to consider putting up a sign outside of your home. If the bustle and noise outdoors is still really distracting to you, upgrade to higher quality insulation that can effectively block out most of the noise.

Complete, radio silence might not necessarily work for you. The quiet commotions from outside might still be distracting to you. In these situations, you might want to opt to put on some white noise in the background. This can be anything from the sound of raindrops to subtle, calming music notes. You can either play the white noise from your laptop or you can even purchase speakers that can only produce a variety of white noise to keep you calm, relaxed and concentrated.

Having a quiet office is much more than just eliminating distractions, you should also consider the type of timetable or work schedule that will work best for you. This is also where your planner comes in handy. Try to schedule in consistent work hours during the day where you'll be largely left alone. For example, if you have young children, your work day should ideally begin when they go to school, as this is when you're going to have the most peace and quiet at home and the fewest distractions. The same can be said for if you have a spouse or a partner. Working during regular work hours can also be beneficial, as the streets will likely be less busy and you won't get distracted by any noise your neighbors might make.

CHAPTER 5: TAKING CONTROL OF YOUR DAY BY KEEPING TRACK OF THE TIME

When your mind wanders, it's easy to lose track of time and get pulled into a vortex filled with distractions. Don't let yourself get blindsided by how much time is passing by as you remain focused on important tasks at hand. If you can grasp time in your palms, you'll feel like you have more control over your day, and you will also be able to make better use of your time. While the chapters above have explored how to take control of your day by creating routines, setting schedules and being organized, you'll also greatly benefit from literally keeping your eye on the time.

Keep Lots of Clocks Around Your Office

One of the easiest ways to keep track of time is to literally know what time it is constantly. Clocks are your best friend, so don't hesitate to splurge on them. You should keep several clocks around your office. One on the wall, one on your work desk and even one by the door. This will help you keep track of your progress throughout the day.

You can try using different types of clocks to see what works best visually for you. While analog clocks are most traditional, some people with ADHD have difficulty telling the time when trying to figure out what time it is. You might want to consider getting an digital clock instead that can quickly tell you the time without you having to try to work it out in your head. If you do find analog clocks to be best for you, look for ones that don't have complicated or complex designs on the face of the clock. The simpler, the better.

There are also many additional types of clocks that have been known to be quite helpful for those with ADHD. You can have a custom clock made that basically shows you what your schedule should be throughout the day. This helps keep you on track. For example, if you dedicate the first hour of your work day to answering phone calls and emails, the surface of the clock will section of the appropriate time in a different color. This way, you'll be able to easily tell whether you're on task or not when you look at the time.

Keep Track of Progress with Alarms

It's easy to get lost in your own world when you have ADHD or get distracted. To prevent time from slipping you by, make good use of alarms to make sure you stick to your routine. Set an alarm for however long you want to dedicate your time to certain tasks. This helps you ensure that you won't get so distracted or immersed in a certain task that you lose track of the entire day. For example, you don't want to be so immersed in designing a new logo that you forget to package and ship orders or answer phone calls and emails.

It's easy to want to snooze an alarm, so that you can get back to what you're doing, especially if you feel like you're on the verge of completing a very important task. As a result, it's crucial that you learn not to hit the snooze button more than once. If you haven't completed a task even after hitting the snooze button once, then you surely were not as close to finishing as you expected. It's time to set the task aside to be completed at a later time.

It can also be easy to tune out alarms if you're concentrated or focused enough. To prevent this from happening, place your alarm on the other side of the room, so that you'll have to walk to it in order to snooze or close it. The mere act of having to walk to the alarm will disrupt you from your task and remove you from its allure. For further help, you can even consider purchasing an alarm that requires you to complete a certain task or activity in order to shut it off. This might be in the form of an app or it might be an alarm clock that requires you to push several buttons on the surface of the clock before turning off. Basically, the more involved you'll need to be to turn the alarm clock off, the better.

Hire a Personal Assistant

If it's hard for you to disengage with what you're doing and take a look at the time once you're fully immersed in a certain task or idea, you should really consider hiring a personal assistant. Fortunately, thanks to the online community, you can hire a personal assistant to not only remind you when you need to get certain tasks completed, but also help you out with your business for a relatively low price. You can ask your personal assistant to give you a call at certain times of the day to remind you that it's time to finish off the tasks you have on hand, and get started with something new.

When choosing a personal assistant, reliability is key to your success. Look for a personal assistant that isn't handling too many clients at the moment, has wonderful references and also lives in your timezone. Once you find a personal assistant that clicks with you, it's generally best to stick with them, as it can be difficult for new assistants to get used to your schedule and timetable.

Depending on the type of home business you are running, you might also want to consider delegating some of the tasks to them. Look over the resumes to determine the unique strengths and skills that your personal assistant has. They might be able to take a tremendous load off of your shoulders, so that you can stay focused on some of the more important tasks. For example, if your personal assistant has experience working in call centers, you might want to reroute some of your calls to them during high traffic hours.

CHAPTER 6: GETTING EXTERNAL HELP

Having the home office of your dreams won't be enough to keep your ADHD symptoms under control. There's no shame in looking for and requesting help from external sources, like from a counselor or a psychiatrist. In fact, getting properly diagnosed is one of the most fundamental steps in regaining power and control over ADHD. There are plenty of different types of therapy and support groups in your area that can help. Don't wage a battle with ADHD alone. You'll have much more strength and motivation with help from others.

Attend Counselling Sessions, Particularly Ones Aimed at Cognitive Behavioral Therapy

Staying accountable for your own actions can be difficult when you are running a business by yourself. It's much easier to hold yourself accountable and responsible when you have someone to talk to or someone to look over your progress with you.

Scheduling and attending regular counselling sessions can really help you monitor your own mental health and determine what's working and what's not working. Counsellors that practice cognitive behavior therapy, in particular, can really help you develop and maintain basic learning principles that can keep ADHD behaviors under control.

Cognitive behavior therapy basically focuses on 5 essential components. They include working on improving the following skills:

- Neurocognitive skills, which basically involve picking up and practicing strategies that help improve memory, impulse control, attention control and planning;
- Problem solving skills, which involve learning how to identify what the consequences of specific actions might be, learning how to manage and solve conflict and figuring out what the best choice of action is when facing obstacles;
- Emotional control, which involves keeping your emotions in check, so that you aren't always acting on an impulse or letting your emotions cloud your thoughts causing you to make irrational decisions;
- Critical reasoning skills, which basically involve determining what your options are and evaluating which choices may be the best based on your circumstances; and,
- Social skills, which involve learning how to interact and socialize with other people. This skillset is particularly important when running your own business, as how you interact with others will directly influence your business' image and how your clients and customers perceive your business and company.

The premise of cognitive behavior therapy is basically placing a higher importance on how you perceive the events that unfold before your eyes than with what happens. Honestly, learning how to control your own emotions and make rational decisions can help not your business, but yourself on a daily basis.

Your counsellor will help you identify the triggers that cause you to misbehave or make rash decisions in life. They will then help you come up with specific strategies that deal with your issues. For example, if you tend to become overly emotional when triggered. Your counsellor might want you to take a break and walk away from the situation before responding. During the break, they might suggest you write down how you feel, so that you can better process your own emotions and the different choices you can make in the situation. It's then important to consider the consequences that follow each action and to make a rational decision that will be best for not only your business, but also yourself.

Group Therapy Gives You the Support You Need

Dealing with ADHD can really be a nightmare and a headache. Often times, your biggest obstacle in life is yourself. It can be difficult to maintain a positive outlook on life and on your business when you constantly feel like a failure, or when you know that your own behavior is the cause behind any setbacks you've had. Don't let ADHD keep you down. One of the most important keys to succeeding is having faith and confidence in yourself; however, maintaining that outlook can be difficult. Your best bet is to look for group therapy or support groups for business women or men with ADHD in your area.

Group therapy and support groups can give you some insight, as to what others are going through so that you don't feel so alone. Talking out your emotions and thoughts with others can also help you stay positive and protect your self-esteem. You don't have to feel overwhelmed by a sinking sense of self. You can also find shelter from the storm from the kind words of others.

Even if you don't have time to attend a support group or group therapy nearby, you can try scheduling breaks and appointments with a trusted friend or family member who you feel comfortable in confiding. Sometimes all that you really need is to just talk things out and bounce your thoughts, emotions and ideas off of someone else.

Try Prescription Medications -- They Help!

Don't hesitate to try any prescription medications that your family physician or psychiatrist might prescribe you. If you have been struggling with ADHD, you really need to get a proper diagnosis from a medical professional. No one can really pinpoint the origin of ADHD. While some medical professionals claim that a slight hormonal imbalance is a likely culprit, as there are actual chemical differences between that of an ADHD brain and that of a non-ADHD brain, others claim that environmental factors are to blame. It's difficult to discern whether ADHD is a neurobiological brain-based disorder, a disease or a condition. Regardless, many people have found that taking specific prescription medications regularly can help.

Prescription medications used to treat ADHD are stimulants. These medications are widely believed to boost dopamine levels in your brain in an attempt to improve concentration and focus and reduce hyperactivity and impulsive behavior at the same time. While most ADHD medications function rather similarly, you might have to try different types of medications out first in order to determine what actually works for you and what doesn't. Each patient responds uniquely to different concoctions of drugs.

There are two different types of ADHD prescription medications: short-acting and long-acting. The short-acting medications tend to have an effect almost immediately although their influence doesn't last too long. As a result, you're likely going to have to take the medication several times throughout the day in order to maintain your focus. On the other hand, medications that are long-acting might take a while to work their magic on you, but once they do, you're going to feel concentrated and focused for the most part of the day.

Some common stimulants prescribed for ADHD include:
- Adderall or amphetamine;

- Ritalin or methylphenidate;
- Dexedrine or dextroamphetamine;
- Concerta or methylphenidate; and,
- Vyvanse or lisdexamfetamine dimesylate.

You and the medical professional will need to tinker with dosage for a while before finding something that works for you. It's important that you monitor your own response to the medications carefully, so that you know which type of medication works best. When trying out different medications, you should keep a record of when the medication was taken, the dosage that was taken, your reflection or thoughts on how the medication made you feel, how long the medication lasted and whether you experienced any side effects. Keep a detailed record and bring the record to your next doctor's appointment to discuss how the medication is affecting you.

While prescription medications for ADHD have been known to be rather effective, they have also been known to come with some unsavory side effects, like:
- Difficulty sleeping;
- Loss of appetite leading to weight loss;
- Headaches;
- Upset stomach;
- Irritability and mood swings;
- Depression; and,
- Nausea or dizziness.

You should definitely let your doctor know if you experience any side effects, as this might be an indication that the medication is not suited for your body. Keep in mind that stimulant medications might not be suitable for those who are also dealing with depression or anxiety, as the medications might make your mood swings even worse. It's important to disclose your medical history and health to the medical expert. Don't try to hide anything.

Tip: Try taking your medication immediately before your work day, so that you can enjoy its effects as much as possible. In addition, if you find that the medication is causing you to have an upset stomach, try to take the medication after eating something.

CHAPTER 7: REMOVING PAPERWORK AND CLUTTER ON A SCHEDULE

If there's one thing that someone with an ADHD mind can't process, it's clutter. When your work office looks like it came straight out of a page of *Hoarder's Monthly*, your mind will start to feel scattered. This can worsen hyperactivity or impulsive behavior. You'll also find concentrating or focusing on specific tasks to be much more difficult. You'll easily get distracted by the distractions lying around. In addition, it's easy to feel overwhelmed or get lost in the vast amount of paperwork that is sitting on your desk. One of the most important things that you need to do is to keep your home office organized and clean.

Set Up a Schedule

To absolutely make sure that you won't put off cleaning to the point where there are mountains of paperwork lying everywhere, you should really set up a strict cleaning schedule. Ideally, you should spend several minutes at the end of each business day tidying up; however, if that's not feasible for you, schedule in a larger chunk of time every couple of days or every week to clean and remove any unnecessary paperwork that might be cluttering your desk. Don't ever put off cleaning even if you think that it's not absolutely necessary at the moment. The moment that you do, you'll find yourself spiralling into a messy oblivion.

Purchase Several Cabinets and Bins for Sorting Paperwork Based on Importance

Once again, having the right tools and equipment with you can make a world of a difference. In particular, you want to keep several cabinets and bins in your home office for sorting paperwork. Dedicate one bin or cabinet to paperwork that is considered to be important and others for those that are of less importance. Categorize paperwork based on which bin that they belong to. You should then organize the paperwork based on what they're used for. For example, you might want to keep all of the paperwork pertaining to a certain client or customer in one folder or you might prefer keeping all of your invoices and receipts in one place instead.

You should consider purchasing labels to organize the paperwork. It's crucial that you organize the paperwork as much as possible. For old documents, consider uploading them to a digital cloud. This way, you can save room in your home office. You'd be surprised at just how much space paperwork can take up within a moment's notice. If you do decide to upload the paperwork to a digital cloud, make sure you choose a secure server. You want to protect confidential and private documents, as well as sensitive information.

Shred Anything that You Don't Need

On the same topic, if you do decide to store some documents digitally, it's crucial that you do your due diligence by shredding any documents that you don't need, especially ones that contain sensitive or private information. Don't just unwanted paperwork in your trash at home, as there are a good amount of criminals out there that do go dumpster diving in hopes of finding these paperwork. They can then use the information for identity theft.

Take the Opportunity to Also Clean the Office

Don't only spend time sorting through paperwork. Dust, dirt and any other types of grime that have accumulated on the surface of your desk, floor or other office equipment can also make your home office look dirty and unappealing. After sorting through the paperwork, take some time to also clean the office. Consider dusting, mopping and even wiping all surfaces, so that it looks bright and shiny.

This step is particularly important if you plan on inviting some customers or clients to your home office in the near future. Nothing reeks of unprofessionalism as much as a dirty office. A dirty office will reflect poorly on your business and will influence how your business' image.

Last Resort -- Hire a Professional Cleaner or Maid

If your ADHD mind simply does not permit you to clean in an effective or efficient manner, delegate the work to professionals by either hiring a professional cleaner or a maid. Have the cleaner or maid come into your office every week when you're not busy or when you are no longer working, so that they don't interrupt or interfere with your business.

CHAPTER 8: CLEARING YOUR MIND BY SCHEDULING TIME TO REST

Reign in your thoughts and clear your mind regularly by scheduling some time to rest. Otherwise, you'll get burnt out easily. Although those with ADHD can easily get absorbed into some tasks, they can also get so absorbed to the point where they forget everything else. When that happens, they often forget to rest and will feel fatigued or exhausted quickly. This is simply unproductive. If you want your business to run smoothly, you're going to have to remember to take some breaks every now and then.

Schedule Specific Break Times Using a Pomodoro

Have you ever used a pomodoro? The pomodoro was initially created as a kitchen timer. It's basically a red tomato-like device that allows you to set a timer. Once the time is reached, the pomodoro goes off. While this equipment was originally designed to be used in the kitchen, many people with ADHD use a pomodoro to keep track of how long they are working and how much of a rest they are getting. You don't have to buy an actual pomodoro, as you should be able to easily find an app on your phone or tablet.

Basically, you set a specific amount of time on your pomodoro for working, and a specific amount of time for the break you'll take afterwards. For example, a good idea is to take a 10 minute break after working on a task for an hour. When dealing with ADHD, a break can really help freshen up your mind and allow you to come at an obstacle from a different angle. During the break, you can either go to the washroom, grab a drink of water, take a small walk around the house or even watch a short video. Do whatever pleases you.

Get Some Exercise In-Between Your Work Day

A good way to relax is to get some exercise. Exercising causes your body to release endorphins, which studies have found to be lacking in those dealing with ADHD. You don't have to do anything too hectic. You can go for a quick jog, do some squats or even some pushups on the floor. A good idea to purchase some weights at a local fitness store and just do some weights during your break.

Doing some exercise will also help keep you energetic and healthy. Many small business owners operating from home neglect to exercise, as they are always sitting on a chair at their desk.

Create a Calming Station for When Work Gets Hectic

When work gets hectic and you start to feel overwhelmed, it's time to take a step back and to just find a place to unwind and relax. Let your mind breathe, and it'll help you jump back into the game later on and become more productive. Every home office should have a "calming" station, so to speak. It's a place where you can go to sit down and relax when the phone calls and paperwork start to pile up or when you feel like there's too little time to accomplish all the work that you have to do. Get away from all of the chaos by creating a "calming" station that speaks to one or more of your five senses. Here are some ideas to help you get started.

Visual Relaxants:

Visual stimuli can help calm your senses. While bold colors and complicated designs and patterns can aggravate ADHD, simple and plain colors can accomplish the opposite. If you find yourself easily overwhelmed by visual stimuli, you want to focus on incorporating visual relaxants in your "calming" station or area surrounded by plants. You can even put up some artwork or paintings if you find that they help you relax.

Auditory Relaxants:

If you find that auditory relaxants are much more effective, consider investing in some high quality speakers and listening to some music. It can really help. Allow yourself to get lost in the musical notes. Relaxing to a song is the perfect way for spending a short break. The best part is that you can relax even when you're not working at home. Just bring some earphones and a device that can play music with you.

Olfactory relaxants:

Aromatherapy can really help you relax and unwind when you need it the most. You can create a relaxing home office environment even when you're working by purchasing some flowers or plants to decorate the place. You can further kick the olfactory relaxants up a notch when it's time to rest and relax with a diffuser. Some of the top scents that help promote relaxation include chamomile, lavender, jasmine, rose and vanilla. Shop around to find the combination of fragrances that speaks loudest to you.

Sensory Relaxants:

If you respond most positively to touch, then your calming area should be made up of mostly fabrics and other types of items that speak most to this sensory stimulant. You can have plush sofas with soft throws in your calming station. Spending some time lounging around with soft fabric wrapped around your body can be all that you need to really unwind. You might even want to install a floating bed or a water bed to relax on during your break.

Naturally, what works for someone else might not work for you and vis versa. It's vital that you identify the senses that need to unwind the most when creating a "calming" station that will be most effective for yourself. No two "calming" stations are alike. You can decorate or design your calming station however you want. In fact, the things that calm you might not be surprising. You might enjoy listening and jamming out to rock music. Some people prefer just sipping on a hot cup of tea as well. It really depends on what your preferences are. Listen to your body.

CHAPTER 9: TAKING NOTES DURING MEETINGS

No matter how hard you try. Sometimes, your mind is simply going to flutter off into space even when you should be concentrating and staying focused. Staying on top of everything is essential when running a business, and you definitely don't want to miss a thing, especially during important meetings with suppliers, customers, and distributors. To make sure that you're on point and that you haven't missed a single thing, you want to prepare yourself by taking notes during meetings instead of just relying on your memory.

Your memory might be excellent, but once you start drifting off into a certain idea, you might have missed some crucial points during the conversation that could make a huge difference. Once again, having the right type of equipment can make a world of a difference. Here's what you need to do.

Record All Meetings and Phone Conversations to Go Over at a Later Time

You might truly believe that you've been paying attention; however, if you have inattentive subtype ADHD, you know just how easy it is to start to doze off even when you're in the middle of something important. Don't rely on just your memory or on written notes. Nothing beats recording all of your meetings and phone conversations with digital recorder. This way, you can easily play back the conversation or the meeting whenever you have some spare time to go over some of the finer details. Recording the conversation not only ensures that you'll never miss a thing, but will also take some of the pressure off of your shoulders during the meeting.

Depending on the legislative passed in your state, you may or may not be able to record the conversation without notifying and getting permission from the other parties first. To protect yourself legally, you want to always make sure you record yourself getting permission. You might even want your customers or clients to sign a contract with you that basically gives you permission to record conversations whenever you deem necessary.

Find a recorder with a long battery life for optimal convenience. Charge the digital recorder or insert new batteries every time that you use the recorder. The last thing you want is the digital recorder failing on you mid-conversation. You should also test out the digital recorder yourself before you head over to the meetings to make sure that the audio is clear. If you don't have enough time to go over the recording later on, you can hire a transcriber to not only transcribe the conversation, but also highlight important parts of the conversation for you. If you've hired a personal assistant, finding an assistant with transcription experience might be beneficial in this situation.

Jot Down Important Notes and Make Them Concise

Although you have a recording of the conversation, you should always keep a pen and pad ready to take some simple notes that can summarize the point of the meeting. You want to make the notes as concise as possible, so that you won't become too distracted during the meeting. You also want to be able to get a good idea of the topics that were discussed by just glancing at the note. Keep pen and paper everywhere.

CHAPTER 10: EATING RIGHT TO HAVE THE ENERGY YOU NEED

ADHD doesn't only have to be treated with prescription medication and counseling. Surprisingly, your diet can also play an important role as to how severe your ADHD symptoms are. If you work from home, you have the added benefit of being able to access your kitchen whenever you want. This means that there is no excuse as to why you might not be eating right. With the right nutrition, you'll also find that many of the symptoms will subside and that you will have more control over your life. Here are several tips to keep in mind when making sure that you're eating right and getting the nutrients that you need to tackle the day head on.

Drink a Cup of Coffee Each Morning Before Work

Although most people often get a cup of coffee in the morning in order to get a little extra energy, you could benefit from drinking a cup of coffee as well, as caffeine is a stimulant that can help boost your concentration and focus for short periods of time. While coffee is recommended for the mornings, it should be avoided at all cost during the afternoon or evening, as it will likely just make you jittery.

You can enjoy a cup of coffee at your local coffee shop or you can make your own at home. If you're looking for a cup of coffee that has a relatively higher caffeine content, then you'll want to opt for a blonde roast rather than a dark roast. Caffeine is thought to reduce blood flow to the brain via vasoconstriction. Some medical experts hypothesize that drinking coffee in the morning helps to redirect blood flow that would otherwise go to the part of the brain responsible for impulsive behavior.

Avoid Eating Sugary Foods and Sweets

Although there isn't any concrete proof that sugary foods cause hyperactivity, some people with ADHD do find that avoiding a diet high in sugars can be quite beneficial in managing symptoms of ADHD. This could perhaps be due to the fact that extra sugar will give you more energy throughout the day. As it can be difficult to find an outlet for channeling the energy when you work from home and spend the majority of the time sitting at a desk, it's best to avoid sweets whenever possible. On top of avoiding chocolates and sweets, you should also avoid drinking fruit juices as they are loaded with sugars as well.

Eat Plenty of Protein

Studies have found that consuming diets that are loaded with protein can help you manage your ADHD symptoms. This might be due to the fact that brain-awakening neurotransmitters are produced by the body when you consume protein. Protein also prevent your blood sugar levels from surging as well. When blood sugar levels rise, you'll tend to become more hyperactive.

You should try to eat as much lean meat that is loaded with protein as possible. Lean beef, pork, poultry and fish are great ingredients to add to your diet. If you're a vegetarian or simply prefer vegetables to meat, consider adding beans, nut, soy and even low-fat dairy products to your diet instead. These ingredients will work just as well, as they are packed with just as much protein as meat.

Get Enough Energy for the Day with a Healthy and Balanced Breakfast

While you should aim to eat a balanced and healthy diet throughout the day regardless, you should play a higher emphasis on breakfast than on any other meal. You need to make sure that you go into work prepared. A balanced and healthy breakfast will give you all of the energy that you need. Make sure that you consume a little bit of protein for breakfast. You can scramble yourself some eggs, add some beans or nuts to your morning oatmeal or even simply eat some lean meat.

CHAPTER 11: DRESSING FOR SUCCESS

If you want to succeed, you're going to have to dress the part. Dressing for success is not only for yourself, but also for upholding a certain image or reputation among your clients and customers. The way that you present yourself can have a profound impact on how others see you, and if you want to ignite a sense of trust, you're going to have to look professional and on point at all times, especially when you're meeting with a client, customer or even a supplier. Don't go into meetings wearing nothing but sweatpants and a hoodie. To dress for success consistently consider the following tips.

Lay Out Several Outfits Ahead of TIme

It's easy to get lost in the whole ordeal of choosing an outfit, especially if you have an important meeting or business event to attend to. To avoid wasting any time and to avoid walking out of the house or meeting a client looking like a nightmare, lay out several outfits that you like ahead of time. In the beginning of each week, spend some time laying out several outfits that you think will work. Write down the combination. This way, you won't feel rushed even if you are falling behind schedule, and you won't have to worry that you put on a chaotic outfit with simply too much going on.

It's great to have a list of what works and what doesn't. Whenever others compliment you on your outfit or whenever you find an outfit that you think represents your personality and still looks professional, write the combination down. Include the type of top that you paired with the skirt or pants, and also write down whether you wore any jewelry with the outfit or not. To make matters even simpler, just take a photograph of yourself on your phone. Trust me. No one will notice if you recycle your outfits and wear the same combination of pants and blazers several times throughout the month.

Stick to Minimalistic Palettes and Designs

The simpler your outfits are, the more elegant and classy they will be, and the less likely you're going to make a mistake and choose an outfit or wardrobe that simply has too much going on. You want to stick to minimalistic palettes and designs whenever possible. A sleek pantsuit with a blazer looks quite professional for business meetings. If not, a simple black dress will always do the trick. You don't need anything fancy, and now is not the time to try to let your creative and artistic side come through.

Don't try to be creative and go for outfits that have complex patterns or laces and ruffles. You don't need to look like a piece of artwork that you'd see walking the runways of the latest fashion shows. In fact, you want to keep it as simple as possible. Look for business clothes that have clean lines and that don't have much going on. You don't want others to be distracted from you. If possible, choose outfits that only feature one or two colors at a time. Don't try to do anything too fancy, or you'll end up with a wardrobe nightmare on your hands.

Create a Strict Dry-Cleaning or Laundry Schedule

It's easy to forget to clean your outfits at the end of the night. You might separate the laundry that needs to be done with a business task; however, there's nothing worse than finding that you have nothing better to wear than sweatpants and a hoodie when you have a business meeting scheduled. To stay prepared at all times, make sure you come up with a strict dry-cleaning or laundry schedule and stick to it. You should do your dry-cleaning or your laundry during work hours if you tend to forget to wash your clothes throughout the week.

If you hate doing laundry, look for clothes that are made from wrinkle-free fabric. In addition, if you're always on your feet and moving about, you should look for clothes made from moisture-wicking fabric like cotton or linen.

Buy Clothes from Stores that Organize Clothes Based on Shade and Color

It's easy to get overwhelmed when shopping for clothes. At which point, you might not make the best choices available. If you want to dress for success, your best bet is to avoid any flashy clothing or any complicated patterns. Instead, try to create outfits that are of a similar shade or color. It'll make your life a lot easier. You'll get a better idea of how the clothes will look like on you.

CONCLUSION

Reign in your dreams by taking control of ADHD and preventing it from taking over your life. The journey to success won't come easy, but with discipline and some help, you'll get to where you want to be. Don't fear failure when starting out your own home business. You'll need to spend some time figuring out what strategies and techniques work for you. Keep in mind that just because something works for someone else doesn't necessarily mean that it will for you, so don't be shy on trying new strategies, techniques and methods.

Dealing with ADHD when running a business is not easy, but it's not impossible. You're going to run into a lot of obstacles, and ultimately, you're going to learn a lot about yourself. Don't let setbacks keep you down and just keep pushing forwards. Sooner or later, you'll reach your target and your goals.

www.ingramcontent.com/pod-product-compliance
Lightning Source LLC
Chambersburg PA
CBHW061448180526
45170CB00004B/1605